Honorée Corder's
MINI BOOK *of*
GOAL ACHIEVEMENT

*Get What You Want
in Record Time*

ALSO BY HONORÉE CORDER

THE *YOU MUST* BOOK BUSINESS SERIES

- *You Must Write a Book: Boost Your Brand, Get More Business, and Become the Go-To Expert* & *I Must Write My Book: The Companion Workbook to You Must Write a Book*
- *You Must Market Your Book: Increase Your Impact, Sell More Books, and Make More Money, I Must Market My Book: The Companion Workbook to You Must Market Your Book* & *You Must Monetize Your Book: Create Multiple Streams of Income, Diversify Your Earnings, and Multiply Your Impact*

OTHER WRITING BOOKS

- *There is No Such Thing as Writer's Block: You Can Unlock Your Inner Prolific Writer*
- *The Bestselling Book Formula: Write a Book that Will Make You a Fortune* & *The Bestselling Book Formula Journal*
- The *Like a Boss Book* Series
- *The Miracle Morning for Writers* with Hal Elrod & Steve Scott
- *The Prosperity for Writers* Book Series
- *Write Your First Nonfiction Book: A Primer for Aspiring Authors*

OTHER BOOKS & SERIES

- *Business Dating: Applying Relationship Rules in Business for Ultimate Success*
- *Stop Trying So F*cking Hard: Live Authentically, Design a Life You Love, and Be Happy (Finally)*
- *Tall Order: Organize Your Life and Double Your Success in Half the Time*
- *Vision to Reality: How Short-Term Massive Action Equals Long-Term Maximum Results*
- *The Divorced Phoenix: Rising from the Ashes of a Broken Marriage*
- *If Divorce is a Game, These are the Rules: 8 Rules for Thriving Before, During and After Divorce*
- *The Miracle Morning* Book Series with Hal Elrod
- *The Successful Single Mom* Book Series

Designed by Dino Marino, www.dinomarinodesign.com

Paperback ISBN: 978-1-947665-39-2

eBook ISBN: 978-1-947665-40-8

SPECIAL INVITATION

Be sure to join the
Vision to Reality 7-day Challenge at

https://honoreecorder.com/7daychallenge/

TABLE OF CONTENTS

INTRODUCTION

Dear Reader,

There is a lot of fantastic information about goal achievement available today.

So much information, in fact, that sorting through it all could be a huge goal unto itself.

Enter: this *Mini Book of Goal Achievement*.

Because your time is best spent learning the minimum, you need to get maximum results *so you can achieve your goal as soon as possible.*

Notice I said *goal*, because for our purposes, I want you to think of one goal and get ready to achieve it! Then you can apply this process to others.

As someone who has spent a lifetime setting and (mostly) achieving her goals (and learning a lot when I didn't!), as well as assisting thousands of others, I've learned a thing or two.

I've summarized what I've learned in this tiny read so you can get the most return on your effort with the least amount of time.

Within an hour, you can feel motivated and inspired to achieve your goal, have a deadline for your achievement, and make a plan to make sure you meet or exceed your target.

If you're ready, I am! Let's do this!

Honorée Corder
Goal-setter since 1975
April 2024

Chapter One

IT'S TIME TO GET YOUR GOALS!

You've waited long enough. You've had a goal in mind for years, yet you haven't achieved it. Why? For a few reasons, but none of them matter today.

What matters is today is the day you're going to get excited about your goal, determine a deadline, craft your plan, prepare your protocol, and *get that goal.*

You don't have one more day to waste, and there's no more time to marinate in your stories and excuses (me, either)!

So, let's get a move on!

The truth is, as I write this, there's a goal I haven't achieved yet. Can you keep a secret? I hope so—because I'm going to go "open kimono" with you.

I've yet to achieve my goal of writing fiction. Since my early twenties, I've envisioned living in a cabin in the woods when I'm seventy, cranking out novel after novel. I've been talking about it, thinking about it, and sometimes even doing a little writing.

But have I finished my first novel? Nope.

I've even lived in a cabin in the woods for the better part of four years—with no novels under my belt.

I have all of the reasons, stories, and excuses, and yet the truth is, none of them matter. What matters is this goal is one I have yet to attain.

My goal is that by the time you read this, I'm leaning into my new daily fiction writing habit because I've done what I'm going to teach you to do.

Here's my Goal Plan, which is the same Goal Plan I encourage you to create for your goal.

- **Goal Statement:** Write the first draft of my very first fiction book

- **Deadline:** by June 1

- **Action Steps:**

  » Step 1: Set up my book for success with pre-planning

  » Step 2: Determine when, where, and how I will write

  » Step 3: Just write until I'm done!

- **Success Protocol:**
  - » Execute my morning power-up routine
  - » Execute my morning fiction writing habit
  - » Execute my evening power-down routine

More on this later, but remember that this is here for reference when it's your turn to get down to business. I want to achieve my goal, and I want you to achieve yours.

Before you can turn the page, though, take a moment and write down your goal (it's okay, I'll wait). You could even open the Notes app on your phone, write it in your Bullet Journal, or text it to yourself.

You don't have to tell me, or anyone else, what it is. Just put it in writing. Then turn the page.

Chapter Two

LET'S GET S.M.A.R.T.

An effective way to make measurable progress faster on your goal is to set it using the S.M.A.R.T. acronym. There are a lot of opinions about S.M.A.R.T. goals. Some people love'em; others do not.

Each letter in S.M.A.R.T. stands for something to help you get clarity around your goal (so what's not to love?):

- Specific
- Measurable
- Attainable
- Risky
- Time-sensitive

For the record, I think setting a S.M.A.R.T. goal is the bomb. This process eliminates all doubt, inaction, and scarcity (of time, money, space, people you really like, clients, and so much more). You may have heard this acronym before, but have you *really* put it to use with regard to your goal? If you haven't, chances are you have several goals that—if you are honest with yourself—are actually just hopes, dreams, thoughts, and wishes. *Now* is the time to upgrade them to a goal you earnestly pursue.

In fact, it's time for both of us to stop hoping, dreaming, thinking, and wishing—and start doing what it will take to get what we want.

(We're in this together!)

Allow me to explain the specifics of S.M.A.R.T. goals. Next, we'll tackle *why* achieving our goals is an absolute must. Then, we'll both be ready to focus on the *how*.

S IS FOR SPECIFIC

A specific goal gets achieved. When a *specific* goal is held in mind, the chances of success are exponentially higher. It is as good as "Done!"

A wishy-washy, "I'm not sure what I want" goal won't be a priority. It's as simple as that.

You'll want to be as specific as possible. For example:

A general goal would be, "Get in shape."

A *specific* goal would say, "I will weigh 149 pounds with 18 percent body fat."

Being in shape is nebulous, so you won't really be sure you've reached the goal. You must define what it means to truly achieve it.

My general goal: "Write a fiction book."

My specific goal: "Write the first draft of my very first fiction book."

Specific goals aren't vague.

I'll know when I weigh 149 pounds with 18 percent body fat and I'll know when I've completed my first fiction book draft. You'll know it, too, because I can show evidence of achievement. Either the goal is achieved, or it isn't. It's entirely black and white; there's no gray area.

I've got my goal; now it's your turn.

Here is *the key question:* What do you want?

Take a few moments and answer that question as honestly as you dare. What you want will become your goal, so get excited!

Once you've chosen your goal, ensure it meets the S.M.A.R.T. criteria, which follow here:

M IS FOR MEASURABLE

Because you don't want a goal that is vague, it must be measurable. Having a measurable goal sets the stage for goal achievement!

> **What gets measured (and attention) is eventually achieved.**

It's crucial to establish concrete criteria for measuring progress toward the attainment of the goal you set.

I used to set a goal and forget about it. No longer! Now, not only do I have a measurable goal, but I have measurable action steps too. But I'm getting a bit ahead of myself.

Once a goal is set, consistently measuring your progress will mean you stay on track. Eventually, you'll get to experience the elation that comes with goal achievement.

Spoiler alert! When you don't consistently measure your progress, you usually don't achieve your goal. That would be tragic!

To ensure your goal is measurable, ask questions such as:

- What action steps will I take to move toward my goal?
- How often do I need to take those action steps?
- How will I know for sure the goal is achieved?

Here are my answers:

- Prepare to write and then write for one hour or five hundred words.
- Every weekday and one weekend day.
- When I've written about 50,000 words, including "The End." 😊

A IS FOR ATTAINABLE

I believe there's always a way to achieve one's goal if they are committed, they have a plan, and work that plan like they're all out of bubble gum (and *really* want bubble gum).

Said another way, if you want something and have set a goal, I believe it is attainable. No arguments, no second-guessing. *You can do it!*

However, there are some exceptions. You can't play pee-wee baseball if you're in your mid-forties (but you could coach the team). As of this writing, women don't play in the NFL. The best we could do is ownership. (Now that's a great goal!)

Yes, there are exceptions, but for the most part, I will assume your goal, like mine, is attainable.

> Here's the truth: **When you identify your most important goal and commit to achieving it, you won't be surprised when you're able to figure out how to make it happen.**

As if by magic, you develop the attitudes, abilities, skills, resources, connections, and financial capacity to reach it. You begin seeing previously overlooked opportunities and possibilities. There seems to be a way, whereas before you got really clear, there didn't seem to be a way.

Once you've set your goal, you've also got to *get moving.* The results don't come by themselves, but they will surely speak for themselves!

To summarize, you must:

- Know exactly what you want,
- Believe it's possible for you, and
- Shake your money-maker (get moving).

> A seemingly impossible goal moves closer and becomes attainable, not because it shrank, but because you grew and expanded to match it.

When you commit to your goal, your self-image begins to expand. You see yourself as worthy and develop the traits and beliefs that allow you to possess it. Cool, right?

That's why getting clear on what you want *and* why you're worthy and deserving really helps accelerate this process. I'm not talking about that in this book, but check out *Psycho-Cybernetics* by Maxwell Maltz for specific tools and techniques.

R IS FOR RISKY

This might be my favorite aspect of every goal I set: making it a little risky! *Risky* means the prospect of going after it will require you to really go for it—and that makes you a bit nervous. You know it's something you want to achieve. You know it's something that's achievable—and you know you can achieve it if you put your all into it. You'll have to really make a go of it, and in the process, you'll learn what you're made of. (Hint:

It's more than you think!) Sure, it will be risky for you to name it, and then do your best to claim it. But again, *you can do it!*

> **Truth bomb: It's always worth it to go after what we truly want because a big goal tends to make us into the best versions of ourselves.**

Make sure your goal is a little on the risky side—you'll surprise yourself when you achieve it—in a great way!

T IS FOR TANGIBLE & TIME-SENSITIVE

A goal is tangible when you can experience it with one (or more) of the senses: taste, touch, smell, sight, or hearing.

> **When your goal is tangible, or when you tie a tangible goal to an intangible goal, you have a better chance of making it specific, measurable, and thus attainable.**

Make sure your goal is tangible or connected to something that is—writing words isn't tangible, but having a final first draft definitely is.

Of course, you've got to set a time limit on your goal, and "someday" doesn't cut it.

GOAL ANALYSIS

Once you've set your goal, analyze it to make sure it meets each part of the S.M.A.R.T. criteria.

With regard to my first draft goal, it is indeed *specific, measurable, attainable, risky,* and *time-sensitive.* The date is just a scant sixty days away. Not impossible, of course. Every year, thousands of writers write an entire fifty-thousand-word draft in thirty days during NaNoWriMo (National Novel Writing Month). But with my many obligations and commitments (all of which I love and are important to me), I will have to move Heaven and Earth to get it done. It's attainable, it's definitely risky (nothing like committing to a goal *in a book!*), and I've got an end date.

To all of that, I say, "Challenge accepted!"

What about you? Have you defined your goal and applied the S.M.A.R.T. attributes to it? When you have, send me an email at Honoree@HonoreeCorder.com.

After that, let's move on to another important aspect of goal achievement: planning for peak performance.

Chapter Three

PLANNING MAKES FOR PEAK PERFORMANCE

Once you've fully defined your goal, the next step is to create a plan wrapped around that goal. You won't perform without a plan.

> **You won't perform at your peak without a peak performance plan.**

I've created a fast, easy, and effective way to create your plan and reach your goals with a Goal Plan.

See my Goal Plan below, then use the prompts on the following pages to create your Goal Plan.

First, my plan. Then, more information about the process of using this fun and effective tool.

HONORÉE CORDER'S FIRST DRAFT GOAL PLAN

GOAL STATEMENT

What, where, when, why, and who: My goal is to write the first draft of my very first fiction novel. I'll write for one hour every morning, from 5:30 to 6:30 a.m. for sixty days, or until I've finished.

MEASURES OF SUCCESS

Unsatisfactory – Finish 25 percent of the first draft (12,500 words).

Could do better – Finish 50 percent of the draft (25,000 words).

Expected – Finish before June 1st with 50,000 words.

Distinguished – Finish the first draft before May 20th.

TASKS

- Identify the premise and do the pre-work.
- Write sixty minutes per day, five to six days per week.
- Schedule this writing time.
- Track words in the back of the project on the WORD TRACKER page.

• Write THE END! as soon as possible!

TIMING

By April 10th: identify plot, characters, and genre.

By April 15th: complete outline/beats and begin writing 750 to 1,000 words per day.

By April 30th: Have written at least 11,250 words.

By May 15th: Have written at least 26,250 words.

By June 1st: Have written 50,000 words and a first (very rough) draft!

RESULTS

June 1st – Finally finished the first rough draft. It was easier than I thought and even more fun! Found out that I really enjoyed writing fiction, and while this one is with the editor, I'm working on my next book!

YOUR FIRST DRAFT GOAL PLAN

Follow this template to fill in your First Draft Goal Plan.

YOUR GOAL STATEMENT

Create a brief summary statement of the goal, including details such as timing, cost, location, etc., to make it real.

> You should be able to feel what it will be like to achieve your goal when you've finished your Goal Statement.

MEASURES OF SUCCESS

A measure of success is how you will know your goal has been achieved and to what degree. You need to make some specific, measurable statements about the possible outcomes. But how do you do that? You have two main choices: discrete or continuous.

Discrete: You could use a "discrete" measurement of goal achievement; that is, you either hit or miss a goal. This is a simple way of measuring success. Use with caution, though, as missing a goal by a whisker and calling that "failure" can be discouraging.

Continuous: Another option to measure success is to use continuous results, or a sliding scale. This method is common in business. A rating system determines how effective an employee has been in meeting their goals (e.g., a scale of one to four, where one is unsatisfactory, and four is distinguished performance).

> **The continuous measurement system takes more effort and contains your own subtlety of thought. The benefit is that it encourages optimistic thinking.**

Perception of "shades of gray" encourages optimistic, non-depressive thinking and diffuses any emotional response to a goal outcome due to the multiple possibilities.

I think this is best explained by an example. Your goal is to better manage your monthly budget and start saving money. What you would "measure" is your monthly bank balance, and your possible outcomes could be:

1. Overdrawn by 10 percent or more equals unsatisfactory
2. Not overdrawn equals could do better in some areas
3. Saved at least 5 percent equals expected outcome
4. Saved at least 10 percent equals distinguished performance

You have articulated what would rank as unsatisfactory through to what is above expectations.

Giving yourself a range of results helps you succeed by keeping you motivated. Also, the top rating may be an aggressive stretch target that will push you to achieve more than you think is possible, and (bonus!) provide a fun challenge.

TASKS

This, I think, is the most important part. List the major tasks needed to achieve the goal, staying high level to avoid getting bogged down in detail.

> Make sure that you are emotionally connected to your tasks, as you will want to do them even when they seem tough or take too much time.

TIMING

Break down your goal timeline into shorter periods with benchmark goals for each date. As you can see in my example, I am checking in on my bigger goal of 50,000 words by pacing myself with a plan to accelerate my word count in the last two weeks.

You might prefer to divide the number of days or weeks you have to achieve your goal into equal-sized pieces (I normally do, too). How you space out your dates is up to you; just allow them to coax you on instead of stressing you out!

RESULTS

When all is said and done, write down your actual results as part of your plan.

But until then, and you'll notice I did this (since as of this writing, it is not after June 1st), write the results you want in the positive, present tense.

BONUS: GOAL ACHIEVEMENT TIP

Speaking of creative writing, here's a tip to engage the visualization portion of your brain and allow it to work on your behalf throughout the entire goal period.

Working backward from goal achievement to your first step, imagine each piece as happening in the "best-case scenario." You can bet I am going to imagine the story flowing from my fingers as if by magic, hitting every part of my timeline early and effortlessly. I'm definitely going to imagine that even when I get stuck, I easily get *unstuck* and can move forward relatively quickly.

> **The secret of working backward is to keep it creative and fun. When you do it well, it virtually eliminates any stress out of your goal setting and goal getting!**

You start by "living in the future," telling the story of your life now that you have achieved your goal, and describing how you got there. This description should contain your tasks, so make sure you make the tasks as fun as possible, too!

It can be useful to have a goal buddy—a friend who is also in the pursuit of their own elusive goal. You can ask each other questions to fill in any gaps in your plan. You'll also help each other spot flaws in your plan and strategize solutions.

Chapter Four

PREPARE YOUR SUCCESS PROTOCOL

Without question, the best thing I have ever done for myself and my business is to define what I refer to as my Success Protocol. There is no way I could have achieved any of my goals without a strict commitment to my customized protocol.

Because I have multiple commitments that are unrelated to my goal of writing fiction, I have to ensure I am always able to perform at my best (regardless of what I'm doing—personally or professionally).

In order to add anything to my plate, this goal especially, I must not only stay on top of my commitments, but I also have to be prepared to be creative. This involves extra energy as well as time and focus.

My Success Protocol consists of my morning power-up routine and my evening power-down routine. For the purposes of goal achievement, it also includes habits and routines that facilitate goal achievement.

MORNING POWER-UP ROUTINE (INCLUDING WRITING TIME)

I've carved out three and a half hours in the early morning to ensure I am at my best and have the time to achieve my goals. Yes, they are early morning hours, and yes, I am in a season in my life where I have complete control over my days (i.e., I'm an empty nester).

Note: If you still have school-aged kids, we are in different seasons. Adjust your goals and plans accordingly and give yourself grace. Believe me, the time will come when you have all the time and energy to pursue your goals (and it will come sooner than you think).

In those three and a half hours, I do these things:

- Mindset work. Reading, affirmations, meditation, and more.

- **Writing.** This is non-negotiable. This is the hour inside of my morning routine when I am completely focused on my goal. When it's time to write, I write.

- Exercise. Also non-negotiable. I want and need the endorphins and endocannabinoids (look the latter up, they are way cool) I can only get when I sweat.

> Mindset work, writing, and exercise fuel my creativity and help me perform at my best all day, every day. When I do them, I am mentally, physically, and emotionally fit—and when I'm fit, I am at my best. When I'm at my best, my goals are a given.

All of this happens before I jump in the shower at 8 a.m., and I'm at my desk for my regular workday around 8:30 a.m. No two days are alike, and some days the wheels come off the bus. And when they do—especially when they do—I know I've still made progress toward my goals.

MAKING PROGRESS ON A GOAL

It just so happens that the goal I'm writing about in this mini book is one I can put into my morning routine.

When I'm working on a goal that isn't included in my morning routine (like generating new business), I am sure to schedule time to work on that goal as often as I need to in order to accomplish it.

If your goal needs special attention, i.e., *time*, pull out your calendar and add some non-negotiable blocks of time in there. Your goal needs it, and you deserve to give it!

One quick example:

I have a bespoke book business—I help entrepreneurs and businesspeople become authors with a "done-for-you" service. To develop client relationships, I need to do a certain amount of networking and business development. I schedule weekly coffee, Zoom, and lunch meetings, networking events, follow-up calls and emails. I can't—and don't—let a week go by without making sure I have enough of those to keep my prospective client list filled to the brim.

While this isn't a book on mindset, I would be remiss if I didn't mention it takes a load off to know I am doing more than necessary to have more prospective clients in my pipeline than I need to achieve my goals.

> Whatever your goal is,
> be sure to overestimate
> your activity and underestimate
> your likelihood of success.

I didn't set a goal to write 50,000 words in one month (like the aforementioned NaNoWriMo process). I gave myself two months to exponentially multiply my likelihood of success.

Give yourself the gift of extra time and effort so you can more easily and quickly achieve your goal!

EVENING POWER-DOWN ROUTINE

The bookend on my days is my evening power-down routine.

Is it just me, or does time seem to go by faster in the mornings? I've found it's helpful to prep for tomorrow today, during the more laid-back evening hours.

About two hours before bed, I have an alarm on my phone that reminds me of all the things I need to do before I go to bed.

Among them are laying out tomorrow's workout and work outfits, prepping the coffee pot and tea maker, and any other tasks that will help me get a jump on the next day. I also usually take a shower and wash my hair (morning time savings: thirty minutes!), and do the other things that will help my morning be as stress-free as possible.

Evenings aren't nearly as regimented as the morning—my goal is to make my life easier in advance. (Sometimes, I even make a special trip to put gas in my car and go through the car wash— anything to save time in the morning!)

SLEEP IS A SUCCESS STRATEGY

I also make sure I plan to get to bed with some time to read *and* with the intention of sleeping to get enough good rest.

I'm unable to crawl into bed and just fall asleep, so I get the pleasure of reading a bit before bedtime.

> If there's one thing I *know* will help you achieve your goals, almost above anything else, it's getting enough sleep.

Who feels inspired to really go for anything when they can hardly keep their eyes open? Not me, and probably not you.

Make sure getting enough sleep is on your to-do list as much as humanly possible. I promise you'll be glad you did!

You'll want to prepare your Success Protocol, *in writing*, in conjunction with your Goal Plan. You could leave your success to chance, but why? Stack the deck in your favor!

We're almost done. I just have a few more insights to share. Come with me to Chapter Five.

Chapter Five

SOME EXTRA SECRET SAUCE

There are just a few more quick insights about achieving your goal. These are golden ticket insights—they allow you to bypass unnecessary delays and potentially accelerate your time to the finish line.

KEEP QUIET ABOUT YOUR GOAL.

Public declarations of goals can lead to everything from unnecessary pressure on the part of the goal-setter (that's you) by others who continually question you about your goal, to (also) unnecessary jealousy on the part of those who wish they could set and achieve such a big, audacious goal and resent you for doing so (and have no problem saying so).

> Unless you are absolutely 100 percent
> sure someone is on your team,
> keep your goal to yourself.
> Just put your head down and let your
> results speak for themselves.

STAY FOCUSED.

It's easy to get distracted. To let other people, things, events, and commitments get in the way of your goal (raising both hands in the air about this one, all fingers pointed at me!) and delay or flat-out prevent progress.

I've found it helps me to look for all of the ways I *can* achieve my goal, instead of letting go of the many things I could actually do!

> The best way I've found to stay focused
> is to write my goal in my journal
> every morning, positively and
> in the present tense:
> *I have finished the first draft*
> *of my very first novel!*

Simple. Easy. Recommitting to my commitment. Then, I do the actual writing.

SAY NO.

Just when I commit to a goal, it seems as though all of the universal forces conspire to see just how committed I am. These distractions come in the form of phone calls, texts, Instagram videos, memes, emails, new episodes of my favorite shows, *new books to read*, and the list goes on.

When it comes down to it, my ticket to ride is always to say, "No." It requires no more explanation.

Example:

"Would you like to meet for [coffee/lunch/etc.]?"

"No." (I also add "Thank you!" because I am polite and live in the South.)

If someone is pushy, I can add, "I'm on a deadline" (when am I not?) and ask them to circle back in a few weeks or months. Usually, they don't, so problem solved.

> Saying "YES!" to your goal means
> you'll have to say "No" to everything
> else, taking time from what
> the goal will require.

Only you can be an accurate judge of what you can say yes to while still pursuing your goal.

Well, here we are, almost at the end. Do you have a goal, a plan, and a Success Protocol? If so, good! If not, carve out an hour and get that part done. It will set the stage for your upcoming success.

LET'S GO!

You now have the process to identify, clarify, and commit to a meaningful goal. Even better, you can achieve it in record time by sticking to your commitment, engaging in your protocols, and staying focused.

It's time for me to get busy writing some fiction. Shoot me an email and tell me about your goal! Honoree@HonoreeCorder.com.

AUTHOR'S NOTES

This is the first *mini book*—a new bespoke book product suggested by Beth Walker, one of my very favorite clients (we're working on our third book together right now).

Even though I've moved into a specialty area—focused on writing more of my own books (including soon: fiction!), helping others become authors with custom books, and mentoring those who want exclusive access to me—my roots are in helping people to turn their vision into reality. So it was fun to circle back and dive into a topic I spent many thousands of hours discussing with my business and executive coaching clients of decades gone by.

If you're reading this, won't you please send me an email and let me know if this helped and how specifically? Did I provide enough insight and inspiration to compel you to go for your goals? Did I miss anything? Please email me at Honoree@HonoreeCorder.com. I promise if you write, I'll respond. I'm right here waiting.

If you want to learn more about my fiction (which will range from serials to stand-alone thrillers to cozy mysteries and even romantic suspense), visit www.HonoreeCorder.com/HCCorder to get on the list.

Happy writing!

Honorée Corder

April 2024

PLEASE REVIEW THIS BOOK

I hope you enjoyed this short book. If so, kindly review it right where you bought it (and on Goodreads, too, for good measure). Thanks so much!

GRATITUDE

Byron, I give a sh*t.

Renee, thank you for reading and reviewing everything I write. You're the best!

Jizelle and Tim, IFLY!

Justin, I wake up every day grateful to have you and Vesper in my life.

To the team that made this book possible (and in record time!), I appreciate you! Karen, Jen, and Dino—you all make me look so good (and help me achieve my goals!) You have my deepest gratitude.

And to my readers—it's an honor and a blessing to be able to do what I love, and I'm grateful to you for making it possible. Thank you!

WHO IS HONORÉE CORDER?

Honorée Corder is a prolific author with more than sixty books (including *You Must Write a Book* and *Write Your First Nonfiction Book*) with over four and a half million sold worldwide. She's an empire builder with more than a dozen six- and seven-figure income streams and the host of the Empire Builders Mastermind, plus she's a TEDx speaker. Honorée passionately mentors aspiring empire builders, coaching them to write, publish and monetize their books, create a platform, and develop multiple streams of income. Find out more at HonoreeCorder.com.

Honorée Enterprises Publishing, LLC
Honoree@HonoreeCorder.com
HonoreeCorder.com
https://www.linkedin.com/in/honoree/
Twitter: @honoree
Instagram: @empirebuilderusa
Facebook: https://www.facebook.com/Honoree

Printed in Great Britain
by Amazon